# HAL•LEONARD
## INSTRUMENTAL PLAY-ALONG

AUDIO ACCESS INCLUDED

**PLAYBACK+**
Speed • Pitch • Balance • Loop

# ALTO SAX
# CHRISTMAS *Favorites*

2  Blue Christmas

3  The Christmas Song (Chestnuts Roasting on an Open Fire)

4  Christmas Time Is Here

5  Feliz Navidad

6  Happy Xmas (War Is Over)

7  Have Yourself a Merry Little Christmas

8  Here Comes Santa Claus (Right Down Santa Claus Lane)

9  (There's No Place Like) Home for the Holidays

10  It's Beginning to Look Like Christmas

11  Mele Kalikimaka

12  Merry Christmas, Darling

13  Rockin' Around the Christmas Tree

14  Rudolph the Red-Nosed Reindeer

15  Silver and Gold

Audio arrangements by Peter Deneff

To access audio visit:
**www.halleonard.com/mylibrary**
Enter Code
6873-0228-9379-1569

ISBN 978-1-4950-9635-8

# HAL•LEONARD®
7777 W. BLUEMOUND RD. P.O. BOX 13819 MILWAUKEE, WI 53213

In Australia Contact:
**Hal Leonard Australia Pty. Ltd.**
4 Lentara Court
Cheltenham, Victoria, 3192 Australia
Email: ausadmin@halleonard.com.au

Visit Hal Leonard Online at
**www.halleonard.com**

# BLUE CHRISTMAS

**ALTO SAX**

Words and Music by BILLY HAYES
and JAY JOHNSON

# THE CHRISTMAS SONG
## (Chestnuts Roasting on an Open Fire)

ALTO SAX

Music and Lyric by MEL TORMÉ
and ROBERT WELLS

# CHRISTMAS TIME IS HERE

from A CHARLIE BROWN CHRISTMAS

ALTO SAX

Words by LEE MENDELSON
Music by VINCE GUARALDI

# FELIZ NAVIDAD

ALTO SAX

Music and Lyrics by
JOSÉ FELICIANO

# HAPPY XMAS
## (War Is Over)

ALTO SAX

Written by JOHN LENNON
and YOKO ONO

# HAVE YOURSELF A MERRY LITTLE CHRISTMAS

from MEET ME IN ST. LOUIS

ALTO SAX

Words and Music by HUGH MARTIN
and RALPH BLANE

# HERE COMES SANTA CLAUS
## (Right Down Santa Claus Lane)

ALTO SAX

Words and Music by GENE AUTRY
and OAKLEY HALDEMAN

(There's No Place Like)
# HOME FOR THE HOLIDAYS

ALTO SAX

Words and Music by AL STILLMAN
and ROBERT ALLEN

# IT'S BEGINNING TO LOOK LIKE CHRISTMAS

ALTO SAX

By MEREDITH WILLSON

# MELE KALIKIMAKA

ALTO SAX

Words and Music by
R. ALEX ANDERSON

# MERRY CHRISTMAS, DARLING

ALTO SAX

Words and Music by RICHARD CARPENTER
and FRANK POOLER

# ROCKIN' AROUND THE CHRISTMAS TREE

ALTO SAX

Music and Lyrics by
JOHNNY MARKS

# RUDOLPH THE RED-NOSED REINDEER

ALTO SAX

Music and Lyrics by
JOHNNY MARKS

# SILVER AND GOLD

ALTO SAX

Music and Lyrics by
JOHNNY MARKS

## HAL•LEONARD INSTRUMENTAL PLAY-ALONG

Your favorite songs are arranged just for solo instrumentalists with this outstanding series. Each book includes a great full-accompaniment play-along audio so you can sound just like a pro! Check out www.halleonard.com to see all the titles available.

## The Beatles

All You Need Is Love • Blackbird • Day Tripper • Eleanor Rigby • Get Back • Here, There and Everywhere • Hey Jude • I Will • Let It Be • Lucy in the Sky with Diamonds • Ob-La-Di, Ob-La-Da • Penny Lane • Something • Ticket to Ride • Yesterday.

| | | |
|---|---|---|
| _____ 00225330 | Flute | $14.99 |
| _____ 00225331 | Clarinet | $14.99 |
| _____ 00225332 | Alto Sax | $14.99 |
| _____ 00225333 | Tenor Sax | $14.99 |
| _____ 00225334 | Trumpet | $14.99 |
| _____ 00225335 | Horn | $14.99 |
| _____ 00225336 | Trombone | $14.99 |
| _____ 00225337 | Violin | $14.99 |
| _____ 00225338 | Viola | $14.99 |
| _____ 00225339 | Cello | $14.99 |

## Chart Hits

All About That Bass • All of Me • Happy • Radioactive • Roar • Say Something • Shake It Off • A Sky Full of Stars • Someone like You • Stay with Me • Thinking Out Loud • Uptown Funk.

| | | |
|---|---|---|
| _____ 00146207 | Flute | $12.99 |
| _____ 00146208 | Clarinet | $12.99 |
| _____ 00146209 | Alto Sax | $12.99 |
| _____ 00146210 | Tenor Sax | $12.99 |
| _____ 00146211 | Trumpet | $12.99 |
| _____ 00146212 | Horn | $12.99 |
| _____ 00146213 | Trombone | $12.99 |
| _____ 00146214 | Violin | $12.99 |
| _____ 00146215 | Viola | $12.99 |
| _____ 00146216 | Cello | $12.99 |

## Coldplay

Clocks • Every Teardrop Is a Waterfall • Fix You • In My Place • Lost! • Paradise • The Scientist • Speed of Sound • Trouble • Violet Hill • Viva La Vida • Yellow.

| | | |
|---|---|---|
| _____ 00103337 | Flute | $12.99 |
| _____ 00103338 | Clarinet | $12.99 |
| _____ 00103339 | Alto Sax | $12.99 |
| _____ 00103340 | Tenor Sax | $12.99 |
| _____ 00103341 | Trumpet | $12.99 |
| _____ 00103342 | Horn | $12.99 |
| _____ 00103343 | Trombone | $12.99 |
| _____ 00103344 | Violin | $12.99 |
| _____ 00103345 | Viola | $12.99 |
| _____ 00103346 | Cello | $12.99 |

## Disney Greats

Arabian Nights • Hawaiian Roller Coaster Ride • It's a Small World • Look Through My Eyes • Yo Ho (A Pirate's Life for Me) • and more.

| | | |
|---|---|---|
| _____ 00841934 | Flute | $12.99 |
| _____ 00841935 | Clarinet | $12.99 |
| _____ 00841936 | Alto Sax | $12.99 |
| _____ 00841937 | Tenor Sax | $12.95 |
| _____ 00841938 | Trumpet | $12.99 |
| _____ 00841939 | Horn | $12.99 |
| _____ 00841940 | Trombone | $12.95 |
| _____ 00841941 | Violin | $12.99 |
| _____ 00841942 | Viola | $12.99 |
| _____ 00841943 | Cello | $12.99 |
| _____ 00842078 | Oboe | $12.99 |

## Great Themes

Bella's Lullaby • Chariots of Fire • Get Smart • Hawaii Five-O Theme • I Love Lucy • The Odd Couple • Spanish Flea • and more.

| | | |
|---|---|---|
| _____ 00842468 | Flute | $12.99 |
| _____ 00842469 | Clarinet | $12.99 |
| _____ 00842470 | Alto Sax | $12.99 |
| _____ 00842471 | Tenor Sax | $12.99 |
| _____ 00842472 | Trumpet | $12.99 |
| _____ 00842473 | Horn | $12.99 |
| _____ 00842474 | Trombone | $12.99 |
| _____ 00842475 | Violin | $12.99 |
| _____ 00842476 | Viola | $12.99 |
| _____ 00842477 | Cello | $12.99 |

## Popular Hits

Breakeven • Fireflies • Halo • Hey, Soul Sister • I Gotta Feeling • I'm Yours • Need You Now • Poker Face • Viva La Vida • You Belong with Me • and more.

| | | |
|---|---|---|
| _____ 00842511 | Flute | $12.99 |
| _____ 00842512 | Clarinet | $12.99 |
| _____ 00842513 | Alto Sax | $12.99 |
| _____ 00842514 | Tenor Sax | $12.99 |
| _____ 00842515 | Trumpet | $12.99 |
| _____ 00842516 | Horn | $12.99 |
| _____ 00842517 | Trombone | $12.99 |
| _____ 00842518 | Violin | $12.99 |
| _____ 00842519 | Viola | $12.99 |
| _____ 00842520 | Cello | $12.99 |

## Songs from Frozen, Tangled and Enchanted

Do You Want to Build a Snowman? • For the First Time in Forever • Happy Working Song • I See the Light • In Summer • Let It Go • Mother Knows Best • That's How You Know • True Love's First Kiss • When Will My Life Begin • and more.

| | | |
|---|---|---|
| _____ 00126921 | Flute | $14.99 |
| _____ 00126922 | Clarinet | $14.99 |
| _____ 00126923 | Alto Sax | $14.99 |
| _____ 00126924 | Tenor Sax | $14.99 |
| _____ 00126925 | Trumpet | $14.99 |
| _____ 00126926 | Horn | $14.99 |
| _____ 00126927 | Trombone | $14.99 |
| _____ 00126928 | Violin | $14.99 |
| _____ 00126929 | Viola | $14.99 |
| _____ 00126930 | Cello | $14.99 |

## Top Hits

Adventure of a Lifetime • Budapest • Die a Happy Man • Ex's & Oh's • Fight Song • Hello • Let It Go • Love Yourself • One Call Away • Pillowtalk • Stitches • Writing's on the Wall.

| | | |
|---|---|---|
| _____ 00171073 | Flute | $12.99 |
| _____ 00171074 | Clarinet | $12.99 |
| _____ 00171075 | Alto Sax | $12.99 |
| _____ 00171106 | Tenor Sax | $12.99 |
| _____ 00171107 | Trumpet | $12.99 |
| _____ 00171108 | Horn | $12.99 |
| _____ 00171109 | Trombone | $12.99 |
| _____ 00171110 | Violin | $12.99 |
| _____ 00171111 | Viola | $12.99 |
| _____ 00171112 | Cello | $12.99 |

## Wicked

As Long As You're Mine • Dancing Through Life • Defying Gravity • For Good • I'm Not That Girl • Popular • The Wizard and I • and more.

| | | |
|---|---|---|
| _____ 00842236 | Flute | $12.99 |
| _____ 00842237 | Clarinet | $12.99 |
| _____ 00842238 | Alto Saxophone | $11.95 |
| _____ 00842239 | Tenor Saxophone | $11.95 |
| _____ 00842240 | Trumpet | $11.99 |
| _____ 00842241 | Horn | $11.95 |
| _____ 00842242 | Trombone | $12.99 |
| _____ 00842243 | Violin | $11.99 |
| _____ 00842244 | Viola | $12.99 |
| _____ 00842245 | Cello | $12.99 |

0617